Exploring the West

Tales of Courage on the
LEWIS AND CLARK EXPEDITION

Written by Maggie Mead
Illustrated by Laura Jacobsen

RED CHAIR ·PRESS·

Please visit our website at **www.redchairpress.com** for more high-quality products for young readers.

 EDUCATORS: Find FREE lesson plans and a Readers' Theater script for this book at www.redchairpress.com/free-activities.

About the Author

Maggie Mead has written numerous biographies, news articles, and plays. A former editor of Weekly Reader's newsmagazine *Current Events*, she is currently assistant editor of Scholastic's science periodical *SuperScience*.

Exploring the West : Tales of courage on the Lewis and Clark Expedition

Publisher's Cataloging-In-Publication Data
(Prepared by The Donohue Group, Inc.)

Mead, Margaret R.
    Exploring the West : tales of courage on the Lewis and Clark Expedition / written by Maggie Mead ; illustrated by Laura Jacobsen.

    1 electronic resource : illustrations, map. -- (Setting the stage for fluency)

    Summary: In 1804, President Thomas Jefferson sent Meriwether Lewis and William Clark and 33 adventurers to explore the vast land west of the Mississippi River that he had purchased from France. This play tells the journey of these brave explorers.
    Interest age level: 009-012.
    Issued also as an ebook.
    Includes bibliographical references.
    ISBN: 978-1-939656-65-0 (library binding/hardcover)
    ISBN: 978-1-939656-66-7 (paperback)

    1. Lewis, Meriwether, 1774-1809--Juvenile drama. 2. Clark, William, 1770-1838--Juvenile drama. 3. Lewis and Clark Expedition (1804-1806)—Juvenile drama. 4. Explorers--West (U.S.)--Juvenile drama. 5. West (U.S.)--Discovery and exploration--Juvenile drama. 6. Lewis, Meriwether, 1774-1809--Drama. 7. Clark, William, 1770-1838--Drama. 8. Lewis and Clark Expedition (1804-1806)--Drama. 9. Explorers--West (U.S.)--Drama. 10. West (U.S.)--Discovery and exploration--Drama. 11. Children's plays, American. 12. Historical drama. 13. Biographical drama. 14. Electronic books. I. Jacobsen, Laura. II. Title.

PS3613.E24 E96 2015
(Fic)   2014944175

Chart on page 5 by MacNeill &Macintosh

This series first published by:
Red Chair Press LLC   PO Box 333   South Egremont, MA 01258-0333

Printed in the United States of America

TABLE OF CONTENTS

INTRODUCTION

In the spring of 1804, 33 brave men left the city of St. Louis and headed west along the Missouri River. They were sent by President Thomas Jefferson to explore thousands of miles of land the United States had just bought from France.

No American knew what the men would find. They hoped to discover new plants and animals and meet friendly Indians. But most of all, they wanted to find a Northwest Passage, a direct route by water to the Pacific Ocean.

The group had two leaders: Meriwether Lewis and William Clark. Clark brought York, a black slave he had owned all his life. Helping to lead the captains were three sergeants. Early in the trip, when one of these sergeants died, the group replaced him with a carpenter named Patrick Gass.

Patrick Gass lived to be 98—longer than any member of the expedition. Old Patrick Gass tells this story in 1858, three years before the Civil War. He has just tried to join the Union Army but was rejected because of his age. (He was 87). He sits on his porch in Virginia with his two youngest children, 15-year-old James and 10-year-old Rachel.

THE CAST OF CHARACTERS

Rachel Gass (Patrick Gass's 10-year-old daughter)

Old Patrick Gass (87 years old)

James Gass (Patrick Gass's 15-year-old son)

Young Patrick Gass (age 34-35)

William Clark

Meriwether Lewis

Joseph Fields

Reuben Fields

York

Chief Weuthe

Mandan girl

Mandan boy

Sacagawea

Charbonneau

Comeahwait

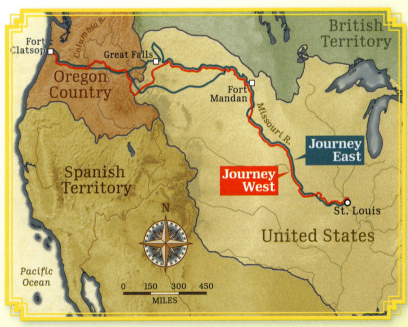

Lewis and Clark's Outbound Route Shown in Red, Inbound in Blue

5

SCENE ONE

Rachel Gass: Papa, is there going to be war?

Old Patrick Gass: It sure does look that way.

James Gass: Are you gonna fight?

Old Gass: I tried to sign up. But believe it or not, the Union army doesn't seem to want an 87-year-old patriot—even though I've been here for this country since the beginning. I remember when the Constitution was signed.

Rachel: You discovered the Pacific Ocean!

Old Gass: I didn't discover it. But I was one of the first Americans to see it.

James: You fought the Indians out west.

Old Gass: James, we didn't fight them. We made friends with them.

Rachel: Made friends with them?

Old Gass: That's right. That was one of the main goals of the Lewis and Clark Expedition. President Thomas Jefferson wanted to know more about the land he bought from France—including the people who lived on it. This country today could learn some things from the Lewis and Clark Expedition.

James: What do you mean?

Old Gass: Well, you see how divided people are today? Our 30-person party included three different races, a woman, and an infant. And we managed to cross a whole country. We made a great team. Do you want to hear about it?

Rachel and James: Yes!

Old Gass: Well, where do I start? Going up the Missouri River, I suppose.

Rachel: You went up the river?

Old Gass: We did. We put our gear in large wooden boats. Some men rowed. Others pulled the boat upstream with ropes. You know, as a carpenter, I was used to hard labor. But pulling those boats about broke my back. It was slow going …

Joseph Field: This river is like quicksand!

Reuben Field: It would help if it went the other direction …

Joseph: It would help if there weren't so many mosquitos.

William Clark: It will be easier on the way back, men.

Meriwether Lewis: The boats will be lighter then too. We've packed a lot of **trinkets** to give to the Indians: mirrors, beads, knives, kettles, combs …

Young Gass: Captain Lewis, when we get out west, what do you expect to find?

Old Gass: Lewis had been Jefferson's secretary. The two of them had been studying the West for years, and Lewis knew more about science than any man I ever met.

Lewis: Well Gass, I've read every book in the president's library about the West and each promises something different. One says there are volcanoes. Another says there are unicorns.

Joseph: Unicorns? You mean them magical horses with horns?

Lewis: Some books say there are six-foot tall beavers and friendly buffalo that stand on two feet.

Reuben: Really?

Lewis: But nobody knows what's really out there. No one has travelled across the country and returned to tell the story.

Clark: All right, men! When we reach that tree there, it will be 12 miles. That's good for a day's travel in rough water. Let's go ahead and make camp. York can lead a hunting party.

Old Gass: Clark was a military man, but he was also a mapmaker. Every bend in the river, every forest and hill went in Clark's notebook. York was his slave.

James: Clark brought his slave?

Old Gass: He did. They'd known each other since they were boys. York was a valuable member of the expeditions: strong, quick, and one of the best hunters. And we treated him as an equal.

Rachel: Papa, were there really unicorns?

Old Gass: Well, no. But that's just the thing—nobody knew. Around every bend in the river, we didn't know what we'd see. It was late August, in present-day South Dakota, when we met two Sioux Indians. We sent some men to arrange a meeting with their chief. While they were away, we dressed in our best clothes and flew the American flag. Eventually, they returned on boats.

Lewis: Men, it is important to President Jefferson that we befriend this tribe.

Reuben: They're as dressed up as we are.

Joseph: But with more feathers.

Joseph: And what's that noise?

Reuben: I guess that's their music.

Old Gass: There were about 70 Sioux in all. The chief, a stern-faced man with a very large feather headdress, stepped forward. The captains began a long speech.

Clark: We seek peace and friendship with your people. We wish to trade with you and learn your ways.

Lewis: But we also must tell you that this land is no longer yours. It belongs to the United States of America. Your new chief is named Thomas Jefferson.

Clark: If you embrace your new chief and country, you will have nothing to fear. You will find we are a mighty and kind nation.

Old Gass: Lewis and Clark then handed out the gifts we had brought, explaining each one.

Lewis: This is tobacco, grown in my home of Virginia.

Clark: Here are the finest blue beads from our skilled craftsmen.

Lewis: These are mirrors. They reflect your face, like a lake on a sunny day.

Clark: We also have the most powerful weapons in the world. Watch!

Old Gass: On their command, the other two sergeants and I fired three shots into the air.

Sioux Indians: (*jumping back*) Oooh! Wow!

Old Gass: They handed out several special coins. On one side was a picture of Jefferson, and the other side showed hands shaking. Lewis placed a three-pointed hat on the head of the chief. Then Clark walked over to an infant Sioux in his mother's arms and wrapped him in an American flag.

Clark: I declare this child an American citizen!

Old Gass: There was a pause. Would they be insulted? Would they be friendly?

Chief Weuche: We will think it over.

Old Gass: That night, we sat and ate together like old friends. We watched the sunset. Members of the Sioux danced around the campfire. The next morning, the chief gave his answer.

Chief Weuche: You have proven your kindness and your generosity. This river and this land will always be open to you. You see, we have been struggling to survive. We have lost many of our men in battles. We are happy to have a friendly trading partner.

Lewis: We are happy we can count on you.

Chief Weuche: But the thing we need most is guns and gunpowder.

Old Gass: Lewis and Clark looked at each other. This was not something they were willing to give, and they told the chief so.

Clark: Instead, we will leave you a translator. He will help you make peace with the other tribes and arrange a meeting with President Jefferson.

Chief Weuche: I am disappointed. But if that is all you can spare, then we will be grateful for it.

Old Gass: As we turned to leave, the chief stopped us.

Chief Weuche: But captains, I must warn you. You will meet other tribes more powerful than us, and they will not want peace. You have opened our hearts, but I do not think, with your beads and your tobacco, you will be able to open theirs.

Old Gass: We gave that same speech to every tribe of Indians we met. And the old chief was right. A few weeks later, we met some unfriendly Indians who did not want us there.

James: What did you do?

Old Gass: We stood our ground. Thankfully, no guns were fired, and no arrows shot.

James: Wow.

Old Gass: But it wasn't all backbreaking work and threats of violence. There was a lot of beauty on the prairie.

Rachel: What was beautiful about it?

Old Gass: Well, unlike Virginia, the land on the Great Plains is perfectly flat. There was not a tree in sight for miles around. When we reached Nebraska in September, you could spot dozens of animals in every direction.

Rachel: What kind of animals?

Old Gass: Elk, buffalo, bears—many animals new to our science. Let me tell you a story about one of them. We were resting at camp one afternoon on the plains—

York: You know what I saw the other day? A tall, skinny rabbit with ears like a donkey.

Joseph: Did you tell Captain Lewis about it?

York: Of course. He wrote down the description and sketched it out in his book.

Reuben: Yesterday he said he saw a strange deer, with feet and horns like a goat.

Young Gass: I've seen more wild beasts in a month on these plains than I have ever before in my life.

Clark: Men! Up! We need all hands on deck.

Lewis: Captain Clark and I have discovered something truly **startling** on our walk. And we're going to need everyone to follow us.

Clark: We're also going to need some long poles and some shovels.

Old Gass: We followed the captains to a vast prairie.

Clark: Now—just watch.

Young Gass: What was that?

Reuben: Oh my! A head—it just poked out!

Joseph: There's a little creature over there!

York: And there! I think it just whistled.

Lewis: It appears to be a village of rodents. They dig in the ground, stand up tall, make a whistling noise, and then slip back into their holes. We believe there is a **network** of tunnels underground.

Clark: We think we could use those tunnels.

Young Gass: Use them for what?

Lewis: To catch one, of course. I've got to send one of these animals back to Jefferson.

Old Gass: We could not believe what they were asking us to do. But how hard could it be—to catch such a little creature? First we stuck the poles six feet into the tunnels. Then we used shovels to dig as far as we could. The animals just kept running away! Hours passed. We became exhausted. Then the captains had an idea.

Clark: We will flood him out! We need barrels of water.

Old Gass: The men fetched the water, and poured about five enormous barrels into the holes.

Joseph: No rodent.

Lewis: Let's try again. Fetch more water from the river!

Old Gass: Finally, we caught one. And put him in a box to send back live to Jefferson.

Rachel: What were they?

Old Gass: We later learned that they were called prairie dogs.

Rachel: Can we get a prairie dog?

Old Gass: (smiles) We'll see, dear.

James: Papa, what about the Indian woman?

Old Gass: Who?

James: You've talked about her before.

Rachel: The one who helped you with directions?

Old Gass: Oh, you mean Sacagawea. She helped us with much more than directions. We met her at Mandan, where we stayed that winter. The Mandan Indians were very friendly. We built a fort there across the river from them. The Mandan were amazed by York. All the Indians were.

Mandan girl: What are you?

York: I'm a man. What are you?

Mandan boy: But what's on your skin?

Old Gass: The boy picked up dirt from the ground and rubbed York's arm.

Mandan boy: Why won't it come off?

York: That's the color my skin is. Just like yours is tan, mine is brown.

Mandan girl and boy: Wow!

Mandan girl: Why are you so tall?

York: Why are you so short?

Mandan boy: My mother says you are Big Medicine.

York: I am not a doctor.

Mandan girl: No! That means you are powerful.

York: Well that's true. Some say I'm more powerful than a bear. Roar!

Mandan girl and boy: *(laughing)* Aaah!!

Old Gass: Sacagawea was a Shoshone Indian who was married to a Frenchman, named Toussaint Charbonneau. But she had spent her childhood with the Shoshone Indians. They lived near the mountains we had to cross. We believed Sacagawea could help us **navigate** the river and talk with the Shoshones. So we invited her, her husband, and her newborn baby to come along. And in April, we set off again.

Rachel: A mother and a newborn baby?

Old Gass: That's right.

Rachel: Did they slow you down?

Old Gass: I thought they might at first.

Young Gass: Captain Clark, do you worry about Sacagawea and her baby?

Clark: Do not underestimate the strength of an Indian woman, Gass. Besides, she sends a good message to any Indians who might see us.

Young Gass: What do you mean?

Clark: How unkind could our party be if we are traveling with a young Indian mother and her newborn babe?

Young Gass: I see what you mean.

Old Gass: Just then, there was some **commotion** in the canoe carrying Charbonneau and Sacagawea.

Charbonneau: I've lost control! The canoe—it's going over!

Sacagawea: Calm down, calm down.

Charbonneau: Oh no!

Old Gass: We looked over and saw the canoe had begun to tip. Equipment was toppling into the river.

Sacagawea: Men, stop rowing! Stop pulling!

Old Gass: Then, with a baby on her back, Sacagawea stepped into the shallow river.

Sacagawea: These are your notes, right Captain Clark?

Old Gass: Lewis and Clark, and all the sergeants kept journals for Jefferson. Sacagawea saved these important records.

Clark: Yes, Sacagawea. Thank you so much for your quick thinking. Another moment and these would have been taken with the current.

Old Gass: Sacagawea also knew better than any of us the roots, berries, and herbs we could pick to eat along the way. She added these to the captains' dinner each night.

Lewis: Sacagawea, this is the best meal I've had since I was eating with President Jefferson.

Sacagawea: Thank you Captain.

Old Gass: The land changed. We passed high cliffs. Miles of waterfalls forced us to travel over land for one month. We were bitten by bugs, our feet were sore and covered by wounds from prickly pear cactus. Many of us were ill. And in the distance, we could see enormous mountains.

Reuben: Those mountains must be twice the size of the Appalachians!

Joseph: And they don't seem to be getting any closer.

Young Gass: Wait a minute. Is that snow on the top?

Joseph: Snow? In the middle of this hot summer?

Young Gass: Captains Lewis and Clark are right. We will need horses from the Shoshones to cross them.

Reuben: And is it me, or is this river running south?

Old Gass: We began to worry. It was already late July, and we needed to cross those mountains before winter. Then one day we got a good sign.

Sacagawea: That wide flat rock cliff—I recognize that cliff from my childhood!

Lewis: Are you certain?

Sacagawea: I'm sure. It is called Beaver's Head. My people come here every summer. They will not be far.

Old Gass: Shortly afterward, Captain Lewis left with a small party to search for the Shoshones. For a week, we trudged along with no word. Finally, on the morning of August 17—

Sacagawea: Captain Clark! Look up ahead.

Clark: What do you see?

Sacagawea: Around that bend, it's my people! I can see them.

All the men: Hooray!

Old Gass: The Shoshone warriors led us to the camp where Lewis was with the leaders of the Shoshones.

Lewis: Clark, men, Sacagawea. I have explained our journey to Comeahwait, the tribe's chief.

Comeahwait: You have chosen a rocky and difficult path.

Clark: That is why we have come here to ask for your help. We are in great need of horses to cross those mountains.

Comeahwait: We'll see.

Old Gass: The captains began to **negotiate** with the Shoshones. Charbonneau and Sacagawea helped translate. But as Comeahwait began speaking, Sacagawea suddenly jumped up and hugged him.

Lewis: Does she know him?

Clark: What is it Sacagawea?

Sacagawea: *(in tears)* This is my brother! My long-lost brother. I did not recognize him at first, for it has been so many years.

Comeahwait: My dear Sacagawea, you have grown up. And you have a child!

Old Gass: The Shoshone women now gathered around Sacagawea and embraced her.

Comeahwait: Captains, we are a poor and hungry tribe. We are neither powerful nor prosperous. But we will help you cross these mountains. We can offer you horses and a guide and whatever else you will need. Come stay with us at our camp.

Rachel: What a **coincidence**!

Old Gass: So you see, Sacagawea helped us in many ways.

James: She was brave.

Old Gass: That's right.

Rachel: She knew what food was best to eat. And she knew the rivers and land.

James: She showed people that you were kind.

Rachel: And she helped you talk to the Shoshones.

James: So the Shoshones helped you get over the mountains?

Rachel: And to the Pacific Ocean?

Old Gass: Well, it was a bit more complicated than that.

Old Gass: One of the goals of the Lewis and Clark expedition was to find a Northwest Passage, a way to travel to the Pacific Ocean by water. But Lewis gave us some bad news.

Lewis: Men, on my search for the Shoshones, I followed the Missouri River as far as it would take us, up to the ridge of the mountains. The view took my breath away. When I looked west, do you know what I saw?

York: The Pacific Ocean?

Young Gass: A river heading west?

Lewis: Mountains. Terrible, steep mountains as far as I could see.

Old Gass: Everyone in the party looked disappointed.

Clark: President Jefferson's great dream of the Northwest Passage is gone.

Lewis: But men, we have a Shoshone guide to lead us over these mountains. The guide, Toby, has told us the route would take a few days.

Old Gass: But that's not what happened. We set off into the mountains with 29 horses and one mule. The mountainsides were as steep as the roof of a house. The weather quickly grew cold. And there was no game to be found.

York: Well, the men and I have been hunting all afternoon.

Young Gass: And?

York: No elk, no buffalo, no grouse, not even a prairie dog. I don't think there's an animal on these mountains.

Young Gass: We sure aren't on the prairie anymore, that's for sure.

York: How I miss those days.

Young Gass: Eight, ten pounds of meat every night.

York: If only we could eat our memories.

Old Gass: We became so hungry, we started thinking of strange things to eat.

Joseph: Did you try candle wax?

Young Gass: You've been eating candles?

Joseph: It almost tastes like honey if you use your imagination.

Old Gass: We were truly starving. And it looked as if our guide had lost his way.

Clark: Toby wants to stop and stay in this fishing camp until he can remember the way.

Young Gass: *(angry)* Does he know that we're trying to get out of these mountains before winter?

Lewis: He's crossed these mountains before. He knows better than any of us.

Old Gass: Toby soon found the path. But that couldn't help the weather. There was rain and hail, and on September 16, we woke up to find …

Joseph: Snow?!

Reuben: It's only September!

Old Gass: It snowed about eight inches that day. It made the journey much harder.

Lewis: I have never been this cold or wet in all of my life.

Clark: The men's clothes are wet and rotting.

Lewis: Yes, and many of them are ill. The horses are starving too.

Clark: And the land is still rocky,

Lewis: I believe the men have reached their breaking point.

Clark: Tomorrow I will journey ahead and see if I can find the end to these mountains.

Old Gass: But just a few days after Clark left the group, we spotted flat land.

York: The end of the mountains! Out ahead!

Young Gass: I see it too!

Lewis: I have never seen a lovelier site.

Old Gass: It took us 11 **grueling** days to cross 165 miles of what are called the Bitterroot Mountains. We were greeted by the Nez Perce Indians, who gave us food and a place to rest.

James: Did people really eat candles?

Old Gass: Candles, tree bark. We even had to eat a horse.

James: How much farther was the Pacific?

Old Gass: Hundreds of miles. But now, finally, we were travelling with the river's current.

James: No more dragging the boat?

Old Gass: No more! We zoomed down the river called Columbia. We met new Indian tribes along the way. They would gather at the riverside and watch us. Some wanted to trade with us. Others wanted to see if the rapids would tip our boat and our goods would tumble into the water.

Rachel: You must have felt famous!

Old Gass: I suppose so. The country changed yet again. In the water, hundreds of salmon swarmed. First, dry desert, high cliffs. Then the tallest, greenest trees you've ever seen and a thick fog. On November 7, the fog lifted.

Young Gass: What's that delicious smell in the air?

Joseph: Well, I'd say it's salt!

Clark: Oh, I see it!

York: Is it–?

Clark: Yes, the vast, blue water is in view!

All: Hooray!

Lewis: Keep paddling, men. The sooner we get there, the sooner we may find food and shelter, maybe even a trade boat to take us home.

Old Gass: When we reached the coast, we saw we were not at an ocean, but a **bay** just a few miles from the ocean. Winter was coming, and the weather had changed, with high winds and freezing cold rain.

Young Gass: Captain Lewis, do you see any sign of traders?

Lewis: The Clatsop Indians tell me that they have not seen traders in many days. Clark went to the ocean to see if he could spot a ship.

Young Gass: That would make the trip back easier.

Lewis: There's Clark now.

Joseph Fields: Captain Clark, did you see a ship?

Clark: I stood on a rocky cliff and looked out over some of the most horrible, violent waters I've ever seen. No ship.

Old Gass: We named the **cape** where we stood Cape Disappointment.

Lewis: Troops, we have reached the end of a long journey across America. We have discovered hundreds of new plant and animal species. We have met and gained the respect of new Indian tribes. We have found the source of the great Missouri River, and we have scaled those enormous mountains. We have overcome great challenges with courage and cooperation. President Jefferson will be proud.

Clark: Now, as the weather grows colder, we must find a place to built our winter fort. We could stay on the north side of the river or the south side of the river near the Clatsop Indians. We could move close to the ocean, to try to find a ship to take us east. Or we could head back up the river to stay near the Nez Perce, where it might be drier.

Joseph: Well, which will it be?

Lewis: We could make the choice, but we believe the decision would be best made by all of us. So we will put it to a vote.

Clark: When we call your name, state where you would like to stay.

Lewis: Patrick Gass?

Young Gass: The Clatsop Indians seem friendly and honest. So I vote we stay on the south side of the river.

Lewis: Joseph Shields?

Joseph Fields: The Indians on the north bank charge high prices for trade goods. So I will also vote the south side of the river.

Lewis: Sacagawea?

Sacagawea: I vote for the best place to find root vegetables to get us through the winter. I believe this is the south side.

Lewis: York?

York: The Clatsops say there is better hunting on the south side of the river, so I vote we stay to the south.

Old Gass: One by one, each name was called, and each person had the chance to state their opinion. By that time, we hadn't seen our families in over two years. We were hundreds of miles from St. Louis. We were even beyond the **boundaries** of American territory. But when Lewis and Clark took that vote, it felt like we were home.

James: York voted?

Rachel: Sacagawea voted?

Old Gass: That's right.

James: But slaves and women can't vote!

Old Gass: They did that day! You see, York and Sacagawea had marched and hunted and suffered and starved like the rest of us. On this journey, we were Americans first.

Rachel: Did you find a ship to take you back?

Old Gass: We never did. We built a fort on the river's south side near the Clatsop Indians. We spent a cold, rainy winter there.

James: How did you get back?

Old Gass: (*smiles*) That's a long story for another time.

WORDS TO KNOW

bay a body of water set off from the main body

boundary the line between two different places

cape land that juts out into the water

coincidence when two or more things unexpectedly happen at the same time

commotion noisy excitement

grueling very difficult

negotiate to discuss something in order to come to an agreement

navigate to find a way to get to a place

network a system of many connected parts

startling surprising

trinket a small, not very valuable item

Learn More About Exploration

Books:

Berne, Emma Carlson. *Sacagawea: Crossing the Continent with Lewis and Clark.* Sterling Biographies. 2010.

Perritano, John. *The Lewis and Clark Expedition.* (True Books) Scholastic, 2010.

Pringle, Laurence. *American Slave, American Hero: York of the Lewis and Clark Expedition.* Calkins Creek Press, 2006.

Websites and online resources:

Go along an interactive Journey
http://www.nationalgeographic.com/lewisandclark/

Read Lewis & Clark's own words, and discover new sights:
http://lewis-clark.org
http://www.pbs.org/lewisandclark/

Places:

Fort Mandan Interpretive Center, Washburn, North Dakota

Fort Clatsop National Memorial, the corps' 1805/1806 winter camp, Oregon